4/8

W9-BGJ-238

WITHDRAWAL

Carrots

By Inez Snyder

Children's Press®
A Division of Scholastic Inc.
New York / Toronto / London / Auckland / Sydney
Mex̶̶̶̶̶̶̶̶̶̶̶̶̶̶̶ / Hong Kong
Danbury, Connecticut

Photo Credits: Cover © Paul A. Souders/Corbis; pp. 5, 15 © Wolfgang Kaehler/Corbis;
p. 7 © Corbis; p.9 © Michael Hewes/Getty Images; pp. 2, 11, 13 © George D. Lepp/Corbis;
p. 17 © Owen Franken/Corbis; p. 19 © Tomas del Amo/Index Stock Imagery, Inc.; p. 21
© Jennie Woodcock; Reflections Photolibrary/Corbis

Contributing Editors: Jennifer Silate and Shira Laskin
Book Design: Erica Clendening

Library of Congress Cataloging-in-Publication Data

Snyder, Inez.
    Carrots / by Inez Snyder.
    p. cm.—(Harvesttime)
    Summary: Introduces the carrot, from the time it begins to grow from a
    seed until it is eaten.
    Includes bibliographical references and index.
    ISBN 0-516-27591-7 (lib. bdg.) ISBN 0-516-25911-3 (pbk.)
    1. Carrots—Juvenile literature. 2. Carrots—Harvesting—Juvenile
literature. [1. Carrots. 2. Harvesting.] I. Title. II. Series.   # Welcome books

    SB351.C3S69 2003
    635'.13—dc21
                    12rdb
                                            2003009092

© 2004 Rosen Book Works, Inc. All rights reserved.
Published in 2004 by Children's Press, an imprint of Scholastic Library Publishing.
Published simultaneously in Canada.
Printed in the United States of America.
1 2 3 4 5 6 7 8 9 10 R 13 12 11 10 09 08 07 06 05 04

Contents

Carrots grow from **seeds**.

The seeds are planted in the **soil**.

5

The seeds have to be **watered**.

Water helps the seeds to grow.

The seeds grow under the **ground**.

They grow into carrots.

The carrots are done growing.

It is **harvesttime**.

Some farmers use **machines** to pick carrots.

The machines can pick many carrots.

Many farmers pick the carrots themselves.

They pick each carrot by hand.

The farmers pick a lot of carrots.

They put the carrots in **baskets**.

The carrots are taken to stores.

People buy carrots at the store.

19

People like to eat carrots.

They taste good.

New Words

baskets (**bas**-kits) containers used for holding things

ground (**ground**) the surface of the earth

harvesttime (**hahr**-vuhst-time) the season when fruits and vegetables become ripe and are picked or gathered

machines (muh-**sheenz**) things that are made to do work or to help make other things

seeds (**seedz**) the parts of plants that can grow in soil and make new plants

soil (**soil**) the top layer of earth that we plant things in

watered (**wawt**-uhrd) to have put water on something, like a plant or garden

22

To Find Out More

Books
Carrots
by Gail Saunders-Smith
Children's Press

Carrots
by Louise Spilsbury
Heinemann Library

Web Site
Kindergarden
http://aggie-horticulture.tamu.edu/kindergarden/kinder.htm
Learn how to plant and grow your own garden on this Web site.

Index

About the Author
Inez Snyder has written several books to help children learn to read. She also enjoys cooking for her family.

Reading Consultants
Kris Flynn, Coordinator, Small School District Literacy, The San Diego County Office of Education

Shelly Forys, Certified Reading Recovery Specialist, W.J. Zahnow Elementary School, Waterloo, IL

Paulette Mansell, Certified Reading Recovery Specialist, and Early Literacy Consultant, TX

Boyle County Public Library